Serapion

*to the memory of
my mother and father*

Serapion

Robert R. Calder

Chapman Publications
1996

Published by
Chapman
4 Broughton Place
Edinburgh EH1 3RX
Scotland

The publisher acknowledges an award from the
Deric Bolton Poetry Trust towards the publication of
this volume.
The publisher acknowledges the financial assistance
of the Scottish Arts Council.

A catalogue record for this volume is
available from the British Library.
ISBN 0-906772-64-8

Chapman New Writing Series
Editor Joy Hendry
ISSN 0953-5306

Some of these poems have previously
appeared in
*Lines Review, Orbis, Poetry Ireland, Chapman,
Northwords, Scotia Review, Spitalfields Walls.*

Cover design by Fred Crayk

Printed by
Econoprint
112 Salamander Street
Leith

Contents

Satires on an Imaginary Republic

Sinfonia

i

'…ringing…'
Mandelshtam

Song
not covetous
touches
various;

never prose its
music sustains
each note sustaining it
continuing
resonant
light…

ii

When what's worth singing seems sunk
in the still echoing swirl,
gone unheard beyond silence
from absence comes an air,
or maybe the one faint note
which seems all music…

iii mattinata

Not eloquence, not a dance,
yellow coltsfoot flowers opened
from thick-stem purple buds in one dirty
Edwardian railway station
siding this Spring morning
above rubbish between the lines.

Morning opens regardless
of whatever affront to feeling,
more honest than words about morning:
and if these scrub-dull waif flowers
know only their moment

it's one which, waiting for overdue,
broken-down trains, poets
miss or at best forget.

Entry

These years' beginnings,
unpolluted still
water in a pool
speak to me of ink,
clear as deep as black,
on which dream, dytiscus
seeks resistance to walk,

untroubled meniscus,
a nib that marks snow breaks
like an upspring's splash
feeding a fish or following
light wings, long limbs, up

risking a word from its dark
sustenance into air.

Telegraph

The bowed line is derelict, dark
snaky rags like bark hanging from
a drowned mouldered sapling
rot off as the snow shows
witches' butter vermilion
like the sun's whiles in skies white
with no spring kind of light.

Rags crumble, drips take substance
on the crumpled slough of a roof;
as the sun gars its ice-and-snow mat
unclot, detained from slipping
it mimics a cloud's slow death
with a frail rain of token
gems that sublime on grey.

Hoarse river-winds shout
a boys' raw, toneless taunt
scorn of the lone flings out:
what can this ruin vaunt?
It answers nothing at all.

Blantyre Weir

What would want to turn into
this contention of branches,
lines awry, each in conceit
of itself as the haze clears off
unbreathed, leaving black and frost,
snatches not song not human,
wood music as branches
cross in separation?

Weighed down by snow weather,
early fragments, not even
stammers or shadows of passion,
strike on the head chilled stiff,
thick as political music;
bud smashed scarting a conifer,
brat not granted attention,
frostsmoke, fleeting, mephitic.

Not the winter chill's glassy laughter
nor giant shadows blacking melting water
and the wedding-dress and shroud upon the ground;

nor as branches wheeze and wood winds whistle,
the hint of bells which delicately tinkles
icicles.

Schwaebisches Maedchen

Like that Indian nun's clothing
you're plain as pure cotton
that wipes old mouths of dribblings,
smoothes the forehead's burden,
cool sheets fresh as blossom.

In drudgery a dancer,
alive, my thoughts are clearer
of weariness from thinking
the cotton clothes you wear,
cotton look you walk in,
cotton of your mouth,
and what I find my peace in.

On the Sound

Seine-netters tied in the harbour's shelter,
a shoal, hulls rubbing rudely together
creak like old over-heavy oak branches
dissenting yet though the foul weather
stops with a desperation on the wall,
can only fling sprays of insults over
and infiltrate snide unsettling currents
round the wall's open edge, round and under
noisy boats.
Kept from a wild sea that rips
its skirt away when tired of the hubbub
some skipper unties, drunk on thirst and hope
drives to open water, lights startling bright…

and then like Diana propeller, keel
rudder start up naked, pitched up rising…
or is it some other goddess, fury,
in that impotent rudder shown the men,

that vain swim their minds turn to as the boat
stands on its prow, up dripping reels headed
down not free.
The fishermen's dry tight throats
long for the bottle, cold loins for the warm,
the birling of their brains for arguments
hull against hull, locked afloat in the bield
they left for this life, this life become then
the fight to be free to be back again.

Primavera

As tired earth, downtrodden,
again turns over,
in the heart a sliver of ice
is burning, *primavera*,

all thoughts, attempts, wooden,
creak, stay as they are,
clear light on old wounds,
life shrinks back to dark

until at last, no escape,
not nails through carpals, tarsals
and the side, a deeper pain
comes of what hasn't happened.

No vermilion flame
or blood – severe serene
Spring breaks in, light streams,
new green.

Evening Song

...at a window in Autumn's crepuscule
white changes, Nocturne, to blue...
thin trees beyond you, piano,
escape your echo,
white hands and music,

brow, full moon in a window
high in the wall,
from night-scented stock and rose fall,
bright-lying sea waves, suddenly
lifting petals, moonlight.

Niet, Ne Pimen?

Towering under the grey-black
stone arch in its darkness
now the door at his back
is again only a trembling
of ancient stone and its dust
dying like a grumble
echoed along the labyrinth
back to the refectory
he moves to resume his candle,
the seat beneath his haemorrhoids
hard wood and his hurried
dinner at odds with digestion.

No quill but stuck with ink
among those stowed and scattered
in a jar or by his pages,
fingers projecting from mittens
grub among each other

to lift a nib to the light.
He thinks it should do, sets it
still uninked to the page –
it smudges dust as it splays.
He throws it under his sandals,
no sound nib and the future's
bloody bleak... barren.

Incongruous as from a bear
the laughing this occasions,
that idiot writing implements
could raise themselves as villains
or victims like in scale
to man his inkwork chronicles.

Some rubbish cut away,
painful attention beading
his beard with a sweat of fever
he nicks a finger splitting
and squaring off the end

of a long feather suddenly
thrust in ink splashing
the way through the fancy capital
to scratch across the page
toward his chronicle's tail,

pausing to not lose place
tracing a continuity
not of the single narrative –
breaking to give a place
to this and that in brevity
making near marginalia
central – as these notes are
if the story doesn't miss.

Talk from the table, tales
as his trencher fought back hunger
creep when he rushes, breathing uneasy
till a belch fetches
soured remembrance
in the midst of mouthed words,
rhythms, phrases
pondered as different
ways from which the work
chooses its little
to breathe in his narrative
half-efficiently.

Gomorrah-on-Thames, 1913

Not the night party less than ninety
years later when a lighter
paid to haul dirt to the sea
ploughed death through a rented cruiser,
somebody's yacht on the river,
a wealthier night-party cruising
the tar-dark slow egg-yolk yellow
lights on the pool of London.

By the starboard rail a baronet,
brandied infant-like larking,
arms flung high leapt over –
so his sleeves swirled white astern
and his host pursued him alarmed
and the cold foul river closed
his eyes, awareness… fetched back
from unminding and from drowning.

Why? Where? He? The baronet?
…and the boat, embankment, air…
Night bit his bones, he resurfaced
burnt by fresh breath through the sheer
mass where the baronet vanished,
heard clatters and shouts from the sober
soldiers employed as the band,
a splash as a man dived over.

ii

Downstream, dawn long past,
a bandsman's white cadaver
is a fishy cold white marble
trawled out of the stream.

The yellow lights were out,
unblown the cold brass rattled,
a ghost's chains, shouldered arms
mourning the musician
ploughed under by the river,
the river, shoulder and shoulder
and washed out sheets of paper,
thought turning over, over.

Roundabouts and Bombs (1914)

Boy-soldiers dream up ripe conquests
another, another... Kakania's
old erotic round Vienna nightmare
where moneyed youngsters learn futility.

The sense of sheer weight
in every Empire building,
dead barocco overload:
terracotta gilded
carefully constructed, heavy tumbled,
oppressive being there – and too in being
weighted mark of a rule too loud-and-mortal:
life overflowing big in dread of death.

For some the ball has reached deciding time:
taper off drink and let the goddess out
some call as unreliable as the being
the item is apparently to serve...
Swilling, lurching, wallowing in wine,
slow as a drowned candle... which is ignited
in throats sung dry to ugly approbation...
The Crown Prince has been shot in Sarajevo.

Like a toper the band falters,
staggers, stops with a blare, suddenly braking
till the reeling leader gets his voice above the crowd,
then the false notes of a high-days village orchestra;
then wine-weariness shaken, a strutting stupor
drilled mechanical does up its buttons.

They struggle half in vain for the solemn march
drunken tongue-clacks beat to nothing. Suddenly
hard soles on the floor start rattling through, into
solemn music that, started off with mistakes,
got speeded up with all this, forced snarled yelping.
'The bugger's kicked the bucket!' some boy guffaws...

a few rounds jump in echo, up and dancing;
the funeral march is brayed out, *forte, presto.*
insensible tacketty boots lift, scart as they crunch
querns on querns on the floor, beyond the triangle's
tinny death grin a cloakroom full of helmets
and sacks, husks for the coming winnow of snow.

Satires on an Imaginary Republic

i Difficulties of a Fixed Identity

Jellyfish stinging them, fingers
drag on the rope as they haul.

Dancing in air netted fish
rise, wide-eyed succession
of the dead long already.

Shouts: boats buck, nets rising
sway with blood in the glaze
as a basket-net gulps, swings aboard

and explodes into the hold
showers on showers cascading
like Zeus' gold under the flares

and even as Danae's primary
gasp is waiting to burst
up slings the insubstantial
soon to be bulged-out net

and as she's being smothered
by what daylight would show mere silver
and not bearing seed of a god

the moon shows between clouds
and a pale white naked arm
materialises below

the quivering wavelet fishes,
the moon's reflection strong,
blue her corpse in our fished-out waters.

ii

Chorus and collusion:
bursting up together
slack mouths open…
fish in the hold
out of the net,
eyes dulling over into darkness.

Not the young fisherman,
away from the water,
a somebody other

looking for the silver
hung up high
back of his mirror,
and his same face there.

From the floor dust sticks
on the shins of his trousers,
his pectorals bruised

with the same quick drop
to the anteroom floor
as the shot went over.

Outside he goes
as planned
to encourage his party.

Rattled in dread his
belonging particles
wonder as ever
whether they're safe from him yet.

iii

Not net, on the balcony dripping
salt sweat on trodden boards,
for fish-silver shards of mirror
sticking in, stinging fingers
and the chin he nestles in them.

The tyrant feathers his fingers,
faking a gesture differently
read – he must be rid of
not the crowd on the square
applauding his comic performance
but these other and minor
mirror irritations
which don't see extravagant emphases,
which do not see, which are maybe
gone almost all, and the hero
of the mob assembled beneath him
is trying to shake from his skin
tiny cuts made into him.

A bang below, round a corner,
a firework to the laugher...
the jellyfish poison interprets
the matter other than that,

and though a man has been shot
by the prating orator's minions
and is to the innocent dead
none such could have existed.

iv

He folds his arms, in spite of still stounding fingers
fancies that moment a nightmare; looks for familiar
items in the room, faces. There is no mirror.

A bullethole, plaster, outside the crowds are dispersing
for a moment he nearly could love their blind reassurance…
until he remembers he can't be dependent on them,
remembers above all his cause, the source of his freedom,
and honour, word by word for what are to him words,
bad poems read to himself he projects on his territory,
stronger as forces than any existing qualities.
Unable to stand his unease he screams for a mirror.

v

A pot of fish stew too heated
rises, brims over, goes settled
as the flames are drenched and perished,
– lift it off, where rest it? –
steamwater splashes down
the drain. Exasperation,
no appetite to eat this
flaking cooling sometime living cod.

vi

The silver of a sick desire,
between the glass and the slughole
a painted-on sheet fantasy of protection,
glass between eyes and the hole filled with plaster,
sand and silver, lead and lime and lies.

vii Battleship Potemkin

An enormous continent's northern water,
north-white light and the city on the shore;
I think back to talk in my childhood
about that old emblem. I didn't go
but some of my friends did, on a school trip
unaware into unholy Russia;

and one of them was standing on that ship
ready to thump a bulkhead with his fist
when not even an official, an intense civilian,
grabbed him very tight around the wrist
and hauled him back from the bulkhead hissing
a gabble all too comprehensible
to a boy with one forearm sorely bruised
who hadn't schemed a crime akin to blasphemy
but chanced on how an idiot tests truth,
finding a hole in what's frail, sacred, rusty.

viii False Spring

I could not welcome that moon's
curious lemon-blue pallor
shining cold on the windows
in the quadrangle's mock-mediaeval
long-ago blackened walls:
the old wars aren't over.

When this now relic was new –
if nothing but a pastiche –
a Tsar held the throne of Moscow,
Lenin was a boy, Kropotkin
living a few miles from here
just up the Clyde in Lanarkshire,

> these cherry-trees hadn't been planted
> that rustle too dry in this Spring
> eerie with night, not pink.

Like waves on shingle, out, in,
the frail ring of leaves brings a shiver,

> froth on winds come out of season
> stings like a nettle soft skin;
> not warming, no rain is coming,

> nothing will break up the steely
> light of those windows whose gleam,
> this moon-lustred black floating evening
> makes elderly stories too real.

I could not welcome that moon.
Dry night-shining blossoms and barren
with a backward call of the sea
shiver some bones in my memory.

And this is the East Quadrangle
of a great nineteenth-century university
in a post-Enlightenment city
implying more than *my* history…

Glasgow 1988

ix Portrait of a Woman

No white night, a deadly bleaching dream
of the scene turned into a photograph
in which one girl's lowered, hazy head
is suddenly lifted up, looking.

Screaming drifts, from her mouth
now frozen open,
the viewing eye given for focus
horror of her eyes' anaemia.

And now – she is no less anonymous
having lost as much past mystery
as a naked cadaver on a trolley,
and shines more stark than a skeleton.

Near nothing I know of that woman
not fixed screaming who was going
to somewhere from somewhere,
save love won't want her pinned pale with fear

in that monochrome of a twilit mirror
where I saw not a soul caught in terror
or as herself. You, me and her
were pictured in the part which caught her there.

x

Small wonder a woman tears
her clothes, a soldier ransacking downstairs
and her locked in an upper room;
> he goes through her gear like fingers through hair
> and nothing can keep her from deaden despair
> save Christ rose from the sealed tomb.

xi memo

How do you know she repeats herself time and again?
Or seems to do that – you who don't stop to listen
or listen to stop, hear your own repetitions;
    you whose nothing ever the same is aye the same nothing,
    change upon change in which ever nothing is changing:
    dry dull glittery sands annul infinite rains.

xii Pan's Lament for the Goat-herd

His ears jut up,
sharp in them kids' cackle,
music seems dead and even
gods tiresome company:

'Daphnis is dead: he
    alone made music dear to me,
Daphnis mastered
    love and died in agony. I
loved him and relinquish
    all – an unformed melody
longing lingers...

Daphnis loved me
    not at all;
in spite of music,
    his own pain,
being torn,
    still tears me.

My feet,
    clumsy
out of the mountains,
    are heavy.
I stumble because I have lost both life and home.
Confused with all the rest in memory
        all melodies roar waterfalls to me,
        and I have no longer any ear or remedy.
        Nor Daphnis' kind due ken of their history.'

xiii

A girl with nothing to wear
but a pair of bare hands,
that might have let her cover here and there;
> her stretched out and dead,
> naked face down without a blemish
> innocently blasted from her bath.

xiv The Tomb of the Poet

In a year of street fights and explosions,
nobody noticed the caving in
of the walls enclosing the space in which
the poet's dead flesh had dissolved,
(the arse just the same as the brain did).

Suddenly his bones were there,
the breach seen by their showing,
recognised by their being stowed
for safety in secret away.

A deadpan atheist's jibe
rose of a resurrection, even survival:
no disproof he's alive
in any boxful of bones,
one man's much like another's.

If some fool bureaucrat brought out a woman's skeleton...
at the time when things were right for a revival...

The joke was consigned to silence
by a wide and common terror,
along with any possible claim to have seen him,
or intelligently critical citations of his intentions.

The boulder had been hard on a door
closed, locked, solid, entire –
it was the tomb had been ceasing to be,
not the seal on its closure.

Fallen in long forgotten,
the poet or that he had died,
nobody looked too hard
at ruins without a sign
of shrapnel, explosion or scorching,

none cared to look at ruin
in the town around when some lull
had lasted, and the air
scented again of green;
for the nose smoke, eyes a skull,
for the skin and ears a dull
monotony from within.

A torch shone round some corner, through a gap?
Might show the poet in wait,
armed with his skull? Or Yorick's?
A head poked into untenanted, undangerous
darkness within that tomb where nobody sheltered?

The calm mouldy whiff of innocent soil
and a few crumbles of timber rotting to nothing
dropping lighter than snow, cushioned by cobwebs
gently adhering occasioned a dread deeper
than the emotional environing with its fear-filled liaisons.

There was no reading that poem
thus no knowing
the sobering wine still in the dead man's cellar.

Now, instead of the tomb,
even memorial
of a founder of a now obscure morality,

ruin, oblivion, common,
the moment's delusions in constant agitation,
the past annulled, no future but illusions
concealing a present of no end or beginning,
no thought, no script, no reading, no
poet.

xv

Fervour for the sake of fervour,
echoes for the sake of echo,
excited long ago and madly echoed:
occasion of echo, object of fervour?

None – a beginningless cavern.
endless roar of a boundless cavern,
dread of such an extent
its generation of noise,
itself and its destruction,
cannot be comprehended, entryless cavern

hollow booming in the head,
and the head won't be fathomed,
lost longing in which the lost are lost...

xvi Presence

The swoop of your bow,
hands clasped attentive,
was never prayer,
only a moment's
passing stone stare.

What stirred those prisoned
clear waters you darted
through with your poison
lightning waft of smoke,
sour sea-anemone?

Only the living fish you now have frozen
to a terrified seeing eye
no life but you
attaches to, flowering
to close on.

xvii Serapion

Under bombardment he walked over the wire
edging his cassock clear of the twists and barbs –
sip-suck sounds of his Flandrish language singing,
rhythmic dartings of light in his hooded eyes.

A few snags snatched, gently he edged it, it slipped
scarcely injured back on his calves and ankles,
brushing the straps of sandals blood and mudstains
dappled as the white, late-washed skin of his feet...
come a mysterious way, through no man's land
he reached the trenches like any sheep in peace
that scouts fresh grazing, dog after its master.

Fair hair clear of his ears, pale face, chicken neck
sticking out of a hole in the clean white smock
that still had only speckles about the hem,
he was never disturbed by an explosion...
each noise however near or loud intrigued him
like a thing not ill or dangerous but another
short-lived entity within creation.

Noise or bullet flying, he gave attention,
and suddenly seemed to remember (what?) when he saw
a bullet vanish within a soldier's chest,
lost within an already corpse or bringing
corpsehood to one yet living. A young boy died
with this unsympathising being looking
through his fading look to behind the eyes
that suddenly lost light, misting with a sigh
unsympathised with, needing no consoling.

There hardly was belief he was walking there,
for no man, mule or corpse over the shoulder
came half an inch above where he was walking
without a bullet. And then he went away,
leaving a corpse which going uttered calm
peculiar quiet sounds, maybe blessings
without emotion, not unemotional,
maybe observations completing knowledge...
finished though none understood, and patiently
without a gulp or lurching gasp or swallow
his face froze white, his eyes went wider, windowed
where they'd been glassless the while he'd walked about
attentive to something none who saw him saw.

Post mortem he had no wings: one broken shoulder
near a distortion of the blade showed a perfect circular
stain, above blood that had seeped under the gown.

The dead face had found interest
in a thing or thought the tongue
had been tasting that instant mortality
the bullet and the butterfly
fluttered through scarce noticing
or if it had known forgetting
the thing it was passing through,
which sank within, sank to the cool of clay.

As if not there, far or away from danger,
the angel did not fall as will a human
thrown by the velocity of a bullet,
but slowly let itself down where it was standing,
let itself out, or let life out of a body
light as it lay unmoving on the clay.

Too exposed to retain life in daylight
a cheekbone smashed and one point of the pelvis,
and other bullets lost themselves in tissue,
and lost themselves for the only form men saw
was the angel as it had walked over the wire,
an other element leaving for print this corpse.

The face broken seemed to contain itself whole
as it had been before, as if in sleep
a smile had come from some taste on his tongue –
not death's, blood's, not a bullet's –
the fact the angel briefly had been human,
when the blood came, his knees bent and he fell,
body not man or angel, into the mire.
No cross, tag, chain round his neck –
unidentified sometime angel –
the pall-bearers asked no question
as they took it under to silence.
To have housed, have been, an angel
was more than enough. No name
was raised over the grave
like so many's whose were effaced.

What was any one of them?
Nineteen, unrecognisable,
mad, saint, didn't matter,
like what the gentle mumbles
of the angel into himself.

He was seen again, not clearly
but surely, under bombardment
or in noise-storms, signifying
not coming madness or death.
How else this story
if it did not mark sanity
to have seen that angel again
in rain above the festering
glabber and shite
oxter deep, digging in
to hold or weaken lines,
or to have seen a first time
faint few tears in its white.

xviii

Dislocated morning, leaving his children awkward,
melodramatic had he announced to his neighbours
he was off to kill the 'father' of their country.
If that hadn't raised a shock from the superstition
that only acts crowds generate can be sanctioned,
one of these neighbours might have started a party:

and his sons might have noted their father's departure.
And even if they hadn't understood
had some knot tied by which later to remember
their lives as they then had been, they had had this father
who had gone out one morning not quite forgotten,
and their life afterwards hadn't been the same.
He didn't set off resigned his shot would miss
and he share fame, lot, in common with numberless, nameless
empty faces behind which little could persist
but rags, clean desolation.
Nor did he shoot for fame
or to fix himself in any inner condition.

He shot to end a sick regime, break a silence,
sow some seed of good, get back to his children,
live long enough to be stable in their later recall
whom he could not other than leave in ignorant silence,
for fear he frustrate his aim, for fear noised rumour
reach the police. He would be no bloody martyr!

He tried to say, I'm going,
things may be utterly different heretofore.
He couldn't get their dirty faces
away from their games to look him in the eye.

They had no concentration for word of their mother,
who very soon would need them: couldn't stand still,
be warned life could soon be a thing of more problems.
His talk was dust to restless childish fancies.

He couldn't have told his volatile wife the fact:
she'd have screamed intimidation,
with tears and talk of children.
He left in desperate quiet,
a thing transpired that morning.

Dead, why did he miss?
Beyond all that morning,
the man went out with purpose and disappeared.

His allies had hidden the gun,
hidden themselves,
he knew where it was in this quiet loaded with men
waiting to come out if ever the shot went home.

Was the rifle bad, the aim?
The miss also was loaded.
Suddenly he was obvious, was running,
Like the ball of rags his sons used for a football
flew from the kicks of bullets, shedding fragments,
away, out of, back in, out of, play.

Another kick out of the ruck, the ball in tatters;
eyes a boy's whose ball will roll no more,
his sodden rags were lifted and flung away.

His children will have wondered, where their father?
He didn't suppose they'd know, wrong answers come too many.
Of his spirit little sign more, corpse in the dark,
his absence from life a factor, far away poem,
he waited for devils or angels to come collect him.

xix In Memoriam Anton Bartusek

This Spring what's manifest
is loss, a great space shadows
don't fill, annulled
in the fresh cleared grove.

He swallows, thunder, flood,
noise, a mass, sheer water,
wordless drowning victim entering
the dumb optimistic silence
of grass till lifeless it rustles:
a future for him null, foreign,
this empty rite kills love.

xx Operation Barbarossa

In the hearth dead ash is scatters,
the crowd and army's burning faces disfigure...
reddened going in the glow, crumbling in the cold,

ash banks, blackened snow,
pterodactyl bones where white-hot clinker
rolled out of the weather...

that burst the cask, the thaw
flooding the cellar leaving
stink and stain behind it,

humanity drying under
ground and looking out
with a child's wild eyes,

pools of drinkable water, rain
troubling the faces it freshens.
Blowing about, storm birds still can't away.

xxi SS Clerk Ordered to Destroy Records (Satyr-Play)

Fastidious, tight, near delabiate
mouth of a gumsy dotard
crimped resenting silence,
spite where the teeth had been.

A soldier had come, young, brutish,
in a van brought to his door
cans of petrol he signed for
and a sealed and dirty envelope.

Buzzard eyes perched (one plays at looking clever)
on the rims of golden wire below his brow
with no patience to sit attentive
in their sockets behind the lenses of his spectacles.

Beak-mouthed, talon-fingered, buck-toothed, a gesture
camp as any aesthete's
slit the flap with a dagger,

laid aside its excessive
polished steel and brass
on a big black classics professor's desk,
the envelope scrunched in one wrinkled threequarter fist,
with free hand, free index finger and thumb

spread out for craning neck and buzzard eyes
the curt ill-typed ink-smudging (rows not in line)
instruction: twelve years' files kept to perfection
recording his pride and what others would deem
war-crimes must without survival burn.

A faint haze formed, a tear ran
like the corner shop cat out and under
the steel shutter closing for night.

There was no sign of buzzard,
the eyelids too were shutting
in the full sockets flickers
like ineffectual kindling or a dying engine.
    The structure tottered slightly, frame shaky
    as the links of the spectacles being disentangled
    from behind red ears by fists full of memo and envelope.
    Whether to fold and pocket them... file the order?

He had not heard the aeroplanes or the alarm.
Emaciated wreck which might remotely
some time since have been human his functions ceased.
Papier maché smoked on a sculptor's wire frame...
    till the reeking stacks of paper caught the firestorm
    full in the face, thorough records of infamy,
    the bones of their recorder, his pride and its home
    after but one genteel pang blown black away.

xxii Skaldic Note

Golden-bristling boar,	yellow metal helmet
beaten prickly,	thick-necked,
	stones for eyes.

Razor tusks	slit flesh like water
separating muscle,	parting like shoals
	creeks dark and shining.

Burning thackit	roofs unite to
drop:	oil-filthied stinking mornings
	night flames made golden?

The Dead and the Living

Like when the eyes are dry,
stinging though nobody's smoking
and a long cigarette abandoned
in a saucer's been burning away,
a white-suited urbane
bureaucrat sham or gangster
has visited, left after him
bleached ash, a bone-bent finger
the least brush shakes to dust,

the squalor in any snobbery
thrives on the sensitivity
that would let such cheap fragility
stay, a filthy infection
rude wisdom flings in the bin.

The Overplayed Flute

Elegant linen-cold white
flute long used, long silent,
tarnished by now-stale breath,
stinking, slightly, and stained
sign of the thing that would bind
(the poet supposedly said);

now sour around the fipple,
keys, pads, hiccuppy sticky
in action, under the fingerpads
powder of mould or crumbling.

The flute's music praised unexamined,
idle, complaisant, corroded.
Fighting to still find music
the head is turned away,
the embouchure held back from
making shape. Breath gathered,
scunnered into nausea,
cannot be given the needful
full note's commitment.
Platitude and a relic.

Frost Clear

Winter smoothes over, frost
works its *Gleichschaltung*
inside the snowcap
and ice's gloss,
teaching a lifeless
conflictless silence of silver.

ii

Frost shines noting only
the glitter of an alleged
reasonable tone
(that keeps the liar on the throne)
till there's only the wind of the tone's play
missing meaning, sublimed away,
shining, biting, blinding empty.

iii

Echoes can drown the sound word, avalanche cover
with snow and stone the dark and the turning flood,
land and walkers;
      the not known forgotten usurp,
louder than the nearer dear delusion
that takes exclusive attention,
             very living;

that near dear fixable or caricatured
with all the surd inaccuracy precisions
of statement hide deny
      as false a present proximate though distant:
modes of the ill-comprehended and incomprehension.

I hate the false exclusive antithesis
between torrents and ice, the easily knowable lit
which makes the obscure sheer dark, just as I loathe
that concept of the sheerly unknowable which the Devil
dressed as death has been granted for boundless exercise.
In my uncertainties I may be wrong, and know.
I detest dark which denies real walkable land.

Russalka

A bespectacled glare through the glass of the tank –
this life a hydrological institution.
No stir but an inverted bottle ingesting
bubbles into air each drip it parts with.

Listening in to out in the corridor,
a great clock's tick sounds out mysterious wards,
every curtained alcove, every drawn screen and
every fear and anybody behind it.

The mood of the clock sounds through the bubbles of air,
a presence disguised, showing imperious yet,
waiting it might be to drown unwarranted birth:
prevent the nymph from slipping out of water.

Russalka, who might not be known now, weep
to veins shadowed by steel struts, locked into crystal
and foster there some soul of deliverance
to beyond the oppressions of this polity;

break the dramatist's beauty of it, tender
bring new live birth out of your drowned nymph's sinking
into difference and finally being
beyond these now past spectres and even free.

The Black Swan, the High Street

Antique lanterns clack
jaws at the man passing;
glower from dim windows
a wick stinking and yellow
has skinned with scorched oil.

Cobbles not muffled resonate
silence, smuts in the wind
and sticky smoke of morning;
the acrid hint makes sleepers
falter in snoring.

Dew's put black on the road,
slippy sheen on the causeys
like spillage out the lantern.
Dawn swells, the road goes smoky
like a wick run out of air.

Pub-signs creak and swing
with a stifled ugly laughter
jingling like bare tills closing
through this nightmare. It's
somewhere else a corpse drops.

Of a Piece with Music

Now the wooden framework's been broken away
the capstone's place where the arc closed radiates
and nothing drops, the vault spreads an equal load,
capstones all each itself keeping the curve up
and open the light built stonework now ringing.
For architecture, music and heaven's above realms only.

The Yellow Carvel

This day's dying is not
by the second or the minute,
this thickening twilight
not on account of the hour,
or of the sun's sinking.

Time vanishes, below –
no count of the drink there swallowed –
through above the ceiling more floors,
joists, a pitched roof, blue-black slates,
to the high miles of thinning air.

Apart from the light in the sky
a thing some time distant comes over,
settles cloud dense on the evening,
and then there's no more wonted stillness
but rising, falling, an ocean;

thick air, clouds in it floating
uniform grey, heavy helmets,
eyes lurid red in the flare
of maybe lightning. Mysterious
drops fall, streets yaw in storm.

But I'm here, a place on the planet,
and whatever superficial
contradictories threaten,
it's a sheer manner of speaking
threw me into the stratosphere
fallen asleep in a basement
bar got up as a ship
years back. Now it's not there

Lebe Wohl

Bleak as a worked-out quarry for all its order
this place seems to me. Its want's not of colour
although the grey prevails there steady and solid:
this levelled place where the natural rise and fall
seems to be lost, all squared, without sudden corners.
Here only drink can hide the want of redemption.

I do not like this place, decerebrate body
that suddenly, when the drinks are pouring again,
will begin to move its arms, its legs, to stagger –
no dance, only the rod-cannonade of rain
hitting flat cobbles, the garlands are all stone,
the gardens' dense summer green cannot be sober.

Autumn's no better, dried brown and russet recall
only a haze of, never the savour of wine.
Winter's bare black boughs find me in a stupor
unable to see them clear, even the frost
and ice can't chill a way into my spirit
beyond a black and white insufficient life.
A souse has the life of a ship in a bottle;
pour, you're still stuck there, pour more, you sink –
a cribbed inadequate language I can't live in.
Sodden with moods, unimaginative squared,
it's you I'm leaving – this critical farewell's
more than the echo of my steps fading.

Scene from a Tearoom

for the Edinburgher cavillt at Edwin Muir's words
on a species o premises he himsel mindit as "nice"

Throu the winnock I saw it,
bidin ootbye til he'd come oot
shauchlin, wan as a corp –
I'd organised the caur ti fetch him hame.

A stuck up auld hen got the Captain
in thon foosty posh Edinbruh tearoom,
him ettlin tae be lowsed fae the shakin
and the stiffnesses and aches o aa thae wounds.

Struttin in black and in feathers
torn aff the dowp o an ostrich
like the billows o some muckle clipper
yawin its wey oot fae Leith,

purpie and green like blawn peonies
her heid-plumes, and owre baith shouthers
a boa speckly wi pheasant, her ae haund
wes haudin up a gull's white feather.

35

A hen in troth, and owre like, tae,
ane swallt oot that suin in ablow her
a fairmer's haund, gallus and gentie
micht finnd the warm round o an egg.

The Captain bestowit nae word,
seemed stuck, but an unco warsle
fae that muckle wrang wi his pins
wes gettin the chair oot ahint.

And that duin, staunin oot straught –
he sweyed a wee, she sweyed back
and a walthy turkey-cock saw thon,
got up, as it thocht, ti defend her.

She soughed, the air washt roun her,
his leg stoun'd, there wasna an answer
fae the Captain – misread as shame.
The walrus was round ti support her.

And the wumman advertisit an ootrage
that got the Christmas denner ti support her.
And the captain got up to get oot,
haein seen, among warse whiles, better.

Look at that froad pretending,
Stop faking thet limp, you craven.
Then a knight got up, ay, a fause ane
fae the Scotch Education Depairtment,

juist as the Captain wes passin –
the thing wes deliberate, I tell ye,
tae gie the puir fellae a shoogle –
I near ran in – it near cowpt him,

owre lamit ti get oot the wey,
and the room soor wi a mutter
wishin the captain could strauchen
and stride oot, wishin him wrang,

them richt, and the sowl faur fae aa them,
at a distance safe for their pleisure.
Then anither officer I kennt
went intil the tearoom bye me,

in uniform, ken, and thae eedjits
admirin him suddentlike turnt,
he was taen in bi the faker? –
that had ser't aside the Captain

but kennt nane o thon palavers
that were on, and recognisin
the "couard" clappit his erm,
and went gey near white as he wes.

Let me out of here, he'd wheezit,
nae mair, juist let him exit,
bury him even, nou brucken,
raither than face such patriots.

Whit uis the brucken heids
and deid friens' courage, them fell,
him aye and on inly bleeds,
gin ye're fautit for cryin Hell Hell.

Hysterias

Nagging inquisitors
dance on a windowpane,
flies in a spider's web
rent by a cleaning-cloth,
still-living carcasses
there since the spider's dead
hang on the draught and lull
till their troubles' long end.

Not shells that could fill
with the thought of some feeling,
neither alive nor dead
since the web wrecked their wings,
idiot heads hang full
of thin blood in vain
as the rain rattles –
souls about to be born.

If only the web tore,
rotted, they'd fall,
guzzle dirt, struggle,
lay eggs, some future
or drop off like madmen
blind to the world,
limbless roll, roll –
somehow have movement.

Maybe their larvae will
crawl and be flies themselves,
nagging inquisitors:
emotions watch me,
raw as I once was,
snatch like small children;
twigs tapping windows,
cobwebs, flies' coffins.

Corbies

Intellect of a black-cloaked University
professor sullen even with himself,
the crow grew thin sitting
on a shell which didn't hatch,
and fell dead from the tree
in despair, nobody watching her;
what starving circling had she seen,
that iron sometime mother,
what cold blood smelled?

Had this MacBeth in his crow's nest cawed
over the cold egg of his lady,
never taken wing with day's drawing in
in the darkness of the wood,
he'd have seen only that enclosed
world he saw, strutting the stage
of emptiness, brushing his nose
as his arm throbbed with rage
as the furies drew in.

The trees drew in round him still,
black numbers in a hard light
which warmed nothing, which no
agony could fade until night
lit up his flying blade fighting
the riddle till he killed and died,
his head high like a sacrifice,
eyes running with moonlight.

Report to the Koestler Professor

I thocht I saw Chris Grieve gang athort Crosscauseway,
like ony Embro ghaist... "Were you aince Huge MacDiarmind?"

"Tho I nevvir shtopped," says he, "I should shay 'yesh.'
Shee: my wallies shoogle juisht the shame azh ever,
and I am azh shertain as ever of my viewzh."

He spied the bress gloff that declares ae biggin the hame o

    THE EDINBURGH UNIVERSITY EDITION
    OF THE WORKS OF SIR WALTER SCOTT

"There izh a shaying: a shmile
  like the bresh plate on a coffin.
That izh a bresh plate
  like the bresh plate on a coffin."

I cried, "I need some air!"

                    "I shall continue!
with
(and shtop trying to transhcribe my deficient dentition!)

    HER MORE MODERN LITERATURE
    MIRRORED IN SCOTLAND'S LANDSCAPE

Claonaig's weedstrung slipway one Saturday in September,
the sound flat, littered with jellyfish showy and stinging,
a fishy smell all about, and highland scenery,
a young buzzard hopping from pole to telegraph pole,
a hantle alien tourists puffing pollution,

clouds across the lift, horizon to horizon,
the view to anywhere from this corner of stony mainland
thoroughly obscured by fog, the small overcropped green land
littered with a lot of shite, come out of a lot of sheep..."

Celtic Intuition

"blanc conflit"
             Mallarmé

Wi a few preliminary coughs
as ae mair smoker wha whiles bibs owre muckle booze
I confess: I've no read Shirokogoroff's
The Psychomental Complex of the Tungus...

which is no why it sticks in my craw,
thon slogan o Conaucht MacAlpen, womb and begetter
o blizzards o windy prose hauf-quotin MacDiarmid,
the cant phrase aft-repeatit, *whiteness descending*.

No seldom ye'll hear thon no-quite-scholar blaw,
uisin yon phrase as an endin, *whiteness descending*,
whaur a great line o the auld man wad ser faur better:
'It's juist mair snaw.'

Then

A white stone shatters the moon,
memory makes of the present
a chilly pool far too soon
ripples, no contentment:

houses fall back, are small
as cottages seen from a mountain.
The grief of young days grows too tall:
a hard climb back from that pain...

It's not crags tearing those clouds
up there on the near horizon;
only clouds and winds can tear clouds –
could the moon be smashed by a stone?

False moon those fools sheer feeling
see in their puddle of weeping,
hear echo on unbuilt walls
sore to tear down as the soul.

The truth in the moon the Persian
poet sang for his lover
lives without moon in the lonely
dove which has no place to land.

Tiger's Tooth

Whiles TIGER McCUE, my father's pal Peter
McEwan retired flyweight boxer would open
his mouth on an iron-grey filling tucked flush
under the gum behind his left bicuspid,
a tooth he'd had attended to long before
1939 and the day he retired from the ring
with an exhibition bout out of his weight
for some trembly swaddies due for embarkation.

Seventy as he was speaking, half his life
he'd worn the piece of first aid forced on his mouth
by a chance illegal swing the amateur
got through on the break to his comrades' relish:
it wouldn't have been right to hurt him, TIGER said simply
(he'd likely repressed a counterpunch crowding inside him)
he'd kept up his guard, boxed so as to please the soldiers.
And showed nothing, to finish harmoniously.

An M.O. saw Tiger sip red off his lip,
took him to his room and said, this'll do mean time
(fitting the thing), said he should see a dentist.
Since when Peter had known no need to replace it.

His pride in himself was like pride in that short-term item
he seemed to suck on in pain from his broken femur:
a bus-driver had rushed up and said, "it's all right,
it was *his* (the absconded car-driver's) fault entirely,

so Peter had said, quietly tholing the trouble.
He collected jokes that had something of knockout power,
a man so small in body there could be but little
else to him but his peace and training in love.

Philodemus

At midnight on a candleflame
they swore fidelity
each to the other.
                    Dawn came,
the blazing light of day.

Teanga

Thighs ache to walk hills thick
with bracken, so the tongue clinging
to itself longs for a deep well
and a wide in which
its music will swell
to fall to a bird and a song
which blue will rise
into clear wide open
light hills and kill
that ache in those thighs.

The Rose-tree Nightmare

Winter darkens… Fear,
roarings fill the air,
insanity, despair…

Bones bob in shallows,
feathers drift in…

Lord, what weather.
My poor rhododendron
in bits in puddles

which as they clear
reveal… what muddles.

Meleager

He fights her birdlime kiss
and her eyes catch fire,
flare, burn him in this
his snare, life and pyre.

(Palatine Anthology, V 96)

Image after Thakur

Loud she threw a curse at rain
for crushing her paper boat,
and her drenched voice pained her
feeling her hate-choked throat.

April

Evening sky white, day
comes weary to her place
and from her clothes' grey
to the glow of a face

aware night is for her no parcel of rest.
The sky colours afresh, child at the breast

filling itself with a soft sleep
sheltered from dreams of love and storm
which make day's woman cry, and the leap
from which a child might be born.

Fliederlied

...and these dried stalks where white
lilac was lace on the tree,
Gothic tracery
speaking peace,
could once bring none to me?

Meeting in Death

Going, give me your blessing,
whatever in me might have been bad;
we can't look into each other's eyes when we're dead.

Dead, our eyes light up our night
burst open big asking why
were we not kinder to each other
when we were alive.

(after the Hungarian of Endre Ady)

Hommage

English only the language
Austin Clarke wrote in,
him singing was never
any English thing:

Martha Blake's matins bell
beats through history
through that poem against
stiff-blind ascendencies.

Feet which miss it totter
round uncomprehended treasure,
march-rigid or tape limp
mark Imperial measure
numbered as clock or ruler.
How can a good man stop
mechanical ways and fool
which drown out the penny's drop?

Hofstück

Dirty water trundles down the gutter
out of a cleaner's bucket, into a civer
a limousine's deep shadow covers,
lifting on its springs then leaving.

Glasses glitter, like sprinklings
of cold on the street, or the breath
turned into drops by talking
to run down the edge of a beard.

Monkeypawed finding and feeding,
architects' glasses, zakuski
wave through the air, release twigs.
Like a cloud's passage a tray's.

Glasses empty, afternoon over,
tinkle and roll in a corner
panelled with oak so weathered
its wounds are in the patina.

Glass frosted withered leaves tug
unavailing, stuck down below.
A limousine stops, opens, sinks beneath
another soused success and shuts and goes.

Ode to the Spirit of Music

Above squalor like some Bengali
cities', here all European –
heart not beating, thumping,
hear the noise in the sky –
> only the sound of traffic
> battering Commercial Street
> shaking the sign saying, here
> Jack the Ripper's final victim...

Some who have lived amid squalor
will as like be shovelled away
like unsold yellow Karalas
dumped on Brushfield Street pavement.
> Fields of brush, of broom,
> lands for the support
> (once there was stock, were crops)
> of a public institution.

Bare as land severer sunshine
cracks, truck- and car-tyre impacted
this brick-dotted parking lot
was big houses three centuries.

Damon the mower, Daphnis
the goatherd, rare Ben Jonson
Roman or neolithic
pre-Englishman walked once
> where survivors of St Bartholomew's day
> built the twentieth century's
> unbombed rubble of the highest quality...
Through the crepuscule's grey...
Glassy crook-eyed giants,
Gotham City Gothick on the move...
to make this longtime refuge for the English
sick and immigrant victims of oppression
(Huguenot, Jew, Bengali, and little money)
prey of that whose lack was signal here
long before the child's desire of being feared
by others grew to the love-killing fear of love...

*

A nice man from Chittagong's watching
his English mongrel piddle,
Last of the day a lorry's
departing Spitalfields market.

Soon nobody's there.
Picking his way to the Mission
the son of a Lithuanian
Jew knows he's alone...
except... of course his uncles
all were Rabbis... *der Gott...*
he fingers like a Papist rosary
the rotted silk of his tie.

Shreds of silk white-purple,
coat Crombie overbrushed threadbare,
scarf cheaper fabric worse
treated, in better condition,
he is taking his soul and tie
and brilliantine slick of hair
to a mission built when his family
was prosperous in another country,
one grandmother proud of her firstborn,
Queen Victoria on the throne...
and they spoke three different languages, none of them English,
for domestic, political and religious purposes.

O ELI... One might talk
about what is in this man holy,
when his mother first saw sea water,
when he knew not where he was living
save Whitechapel had a theatre,
market,
Delicatessen.

No fatter than his mother's
older brother's fountain-pen
(an innovation those days)
but twice as long, twisted:
he watched it rise from the jar
as if the fingers and prongs
that compassed its elevation
were performing ritual acts
round a thing which happens of itself

(disguising the live activity of the holy
to preserve some faith in the operations of nature).

Oh this was the mystical
elevation of a peculiar
kinked and stunted cucumber
from the biblical-fragrant liquor of the pickle.

And he'd put it to his mouth
with a meed of exaltation
like the tongue of Martha Blake
of Dublin dissolving in the wafer.
And miraculously re-forming
for the uttering of praises,
and the swallowing of dry biscuits and of tay.

These were days before his voice
(well he had treated it)
moved like the Finger of God
(or like the long green pickle,
its wrinklings, kinks, twists harvested
on the very eve of first frosts,
out of the heavenly liquor)
him
into the Yiddisher theatre.

Would he wonder whether he had mistaken The Pickle for God,
and a voice like his unmistakeably for God
according to the holiest of his relatives
fostering confusion more on their part than on his own
that his own voice was God, and so surely His servant
there was no doubting, no not going into The Theatre.

Why did the foolish so swoon before his singing,
phrasing this way and that, however it pleased him
to treat a song as the servant of near to omnipotence?
What could he know that he could not or would not do, singing?
This was the natural thing, like the women he lived off –
sure he had money, champagne: they were more the providers.
And as the theatre closed and he'd nowhere to go to,
what tragedy in that his voice had failed that year too.

Everything was natural, women like leaves fell,
the benefit of the spring dried up like champagne;
the good meals too – they closed that Delicatessen
but as a boy who'd interpreted English for his relatives

he'd got there early, fifty years before the end,
and collected the pickle and let it do what it had to:
of its nature it had had itself in his mouth
arranged its own being eaten. In his mouth. *Wunder.*

He still had the Crombie… but where get a good brush now
the shops he'd known as the best were all over shut up,
and after their closure decayed, and when they had decayed
so far down the road had been all taken off like a corpse.
One wouldn't go into such shops, as cadavers unkosher.

He was going to collect a tin of Heinz tomato,
only the best would do: as his tie must be silk
then there was nothing in its corrupted condition.
(The soul of the thing is the quality you pay for).
                                      Same for the Crombie.
He had come on a Charity shop when walking one morning.
It would have been good had he been able to spend
                                    his little for necessities
in a shop whose profits were destined to deal men benefit.
And his eyes lit up – new Crombie, marvellous garment
in a new condition
he would have been proud, at any time, to wear.
How his face had lit up when he saw he could not afford it!

The joy of coming on quality, and the sacrifice.
No-one begins with old rags, only a few men are born old,
and the holiness of one's own hardly affordable
rags peeling off one's shoulders.
And Heinz tomato the very best of all tinned soups!

He would feast!
He ate second-rate victuals,
worse than he'd maybe have had
if when the best Delicatessen had closed
he had been content to frequent its nearly peers.

(They were better, in fact, said women, if best in its day
the place his eyes had preferred, like those of his mother,
had been snooty, only, quite fair though far too expensive
if you were stupid enough to bother. Why strive to pay more
when you can get better elsewhere cheaper?)

But he'd have the once best were it only the best potato
or a loaf so stale it was fresh when his mother was alive.

His flat they had demolished when he was evicted.
(What use was there in the place once he was gone?)
From pawning and sales he had still some shillings buried
in a Paisley pattern handkerchief in his jacket,
one of whose broad lapels he one night was admiring,
belle mouton in sheep's-clothes fashion, when it detached.
Thus he also had a prepared sermon on safety-pins.
What once served him ideally he thence for all time lauded.

Such meditations too seldom rose in great number.
Some of the time he perplexed himself wondering why
he was wondering why without knowing the what of why what.

Which diminished by not one unit (the biblical units
he could not remember, ell, cubit in English translation
and so forth...

He thought of a thing by a passage whose rhythm
still came into his head, so that his religion...
and he shaved with an old open razor honed white with art...
was wordless entirely of rhythms; so that his singing,
threadbare voice overbrushed never one note forced,
would suddenly wave in the air. And he found himself singing
ELI, ELI, an orchestra, tears to his eyes.
He knew not how those words came into his music,
and meanings into his mood – what was making this tune?

So that one nice young lady, a nurse
it seemed since some uniform showed underneath her raincoat,
which was unfortunately of no extraordinary quality
had one day been crossing was it Commercial Street
between Calvin Street and Fleur de Lis,
and had been stopped by the sight
of far-worn not-quite-antique Gents outfitting in convulsions:

grief from his diaphragm's dome to the bottom of hell,
and the epicentre of this solitary earthquake
heart under a purple silk tie soaked black with long tears.
In the midst of incomprehensible drowned vocables,
he said to her *mein Gott* is such *schoen schoen* singing,
The God and Beauty such sudden-*daimonisch* song).

(Spitalfields, London E1)

Stanzas from Ibn Arabi

Grey doves fluttering restless with lust –
like them my feelings as I must suffer
unable to remember her face,
her name, and those eyes of hers which alone
fetched light to me.

You ruins here, remind me she existed,
tell about the women you have seen and watched,
the easy graceful movement of their breasts;
speak to me ribs about the deer
which browsed about you.

Tall she stood like the sun and therefore
black night is her not being here now;
and my sole horizon is these ruins
and the scattered fires dawn douses,
and daylight floods.

Draw rein, you ahead of me leading,
lean back in your saddle, let me look
at her and what her dwelling is today;
and when you come to be where she is,
stand there and mourn me.

Here, though, together, let's shed tears,
till all that's happened has been remembered
in each of us. Fertile, dangerous,
without arrow or spear all too soon
this place will kill itself with green.

Will you join with me and with her,
lament the Fall and his lowly state
now walking the way of a poet;
and let me know which country
this is we're wandering.

(after the Arabic)

Thinking

The voice born in the reed cut from its Nile bed – 'the song,
words, most recognise
   are echoings only of sentiments all their own;
   pain, wit and passion, wise not confused to emptiness,
   are dry bone' –
the reed which was discarded, severed and not dead...

(parody after the Persian)

'Land and Sea Churned by War and Storm'

Yet again we're living in times
gone mad: can I have some wine!
(... but I want, really, her eyes.)

Fortune is bread, rolled in a ball...
by tired fingers
that let it fall.

Yet still, if you kindle a flame
it might...
(give some soul light).

Earth's a betrayer, the night's enormous,
and what'll be born come dawn?
Fill up my tumbler, come on!

(after the Arabic)

Message to the Proprietor

'That you're God, that I am an angel
and that this is Heaven, you think,'
to his lord, powerful, invisible,
said the horse, 'since no mere animal
could endure this mess of a stall
with flies swimming round in the stink.'

(after a poem found in a mystical anthology)

Love in the Abstract

Can even the soundest or loftiest notion
know anything of the contingent human being
who, their mind in a fixed state, is its possession?

Does this dulling of my late perplexity,
some time now since she was with me,
say the her I thought me with just could not be?

Is that stranger now with her with another stranger,
and was there ever more than two bare dice
bounced in a bag, and thrown, to us two together?

"We...ll, yes *and* no" is maybe not nonsense if now
I now do know her and the pang left is better not dismissed,
and know I didn't have her and so didn't lose her,

nor she lose me: *undiscovered from undiscovered
parted a while back.* Yet another pang comes: emotion's
so abstract... I wish we could have met each other!

                    (variation on an Arab poem)

Under the Dropper

Missing fifteen seconds' blinking,
the eye the drip's in suddenly
working its lid the quicker's
no longer itchy with grit.

Cool through a blur and flutterings
sight like of day's beginning
of, the dropper back inside,
the bottle being stoppered.

Focus comes back sharp in part,
tholing the hint of a scratch
in the rim of the near recompleted
picture duller but healing.

Stone Pool

Grief can be a hiding place for light.
I remember your eyes rebelled
when I tried some assuagement
of anguish that seemed then beauty,
rock-weeds, a lava shore,
my words ran off and back.

Not make sense fade not lessen
apprehension of lights,
forever a blue-eyed pool
immune to help, harm, changing,
your own set hold on life
a dark sore holding.

More than ourselves our time,
deaf, dumb, the clear stone pool
your eyes and talk so quiet
remind me of as I think to
the cold early of sunlight
not broken through to warm
the day of your enclosure.

Hoffmann Muse

Kaetzchen's gait's a dancer's
some love holds together,
billowing loose-cut trousers
sweep her round each corner
careless what she'll find there.

The sail that shifts like water,
final, quick, decisive
rush for resolution
in fugues her fingers manage;
she is a dreadful driver!

Where what drives her comes from,
who her goddess is...(?), her feet are
clicking round the spiral staircase
as the catches on the rigging
hit the mast – the sail is lifting.

Filled with Bach's B minor Prelude
Kaetzchen's feet and fingers conjure
squally sails to bring her breathing
through the theme, her prow once dipping
coming up to show her smile

and the sail will split with jostling
winds which twist and turn her feelings;
back she'll tow the boat to harbour
rope in teeth, a tireless swimmer
legs and arms forever swinging
slowed by only what she's hauling.

Soon she'll draw it from the water
labouring to get in order
planks and rigging, mast, sail, Kaetzchen
stride ecstatic resolutions
till the nave's a wood of pillars
and the vault's the very sky.

Plaint

No pout pursed nor brow
drawn down counselling fear
or finger stapling your lips
can warn or beguile my quiet

since you always show me these
and discouragement forbye,
to make me regret the said
and the unsaid equally, numb

as if I shouldn't have spoken
when I did, or played dumb
other times… as if
I had at no time experienced,

must never pay attention to,
my own criticisms' promptings;
must heed but your reception
of my words by mistranslation.

Why are you so bothered at
my confident seeming calm?

(echoing Francisco de Quevedo)

Dissonance

(one of the moods)

The doll puts paint on her body,
body slowly empties of colour,
    says Kabir, and a Brahmin grows his hair long
    and in consequence looks like a goat;
    who wanted to write you a song
    which would catch you by the throat?

Only a song would do,
a bird, simple, elusive,
    to fly in to your room,
    perch on your breasts as you sleep;
    sing unrest in its silent
    working there with its feet.

And then you'd begin to dream,
a moth would fly from your mouth;
    that bird would catch it quick,
    your breathing heavy with pain
    as it with your dream in its beak
    flew stormily back and again,
joined your would-be serenader
waiting like a conspirator;
    who'd let it release your dream,
    moth fluttering back to your throat,
    to the bed of a painted doll
    from a tethered weatherbeaten goat.

Patience

Rumpled shapes of Breton
women's caps in a Gauguin,
these roses too much sun
has by now dam' near done in.

Don't just fling them away;
give them, they still have their scent,
a vase for the rest of the day,
a drink, a chance. Relent

and maybe they'll have time yet
if their heads don't nod and shrink
to open before they've upset
and dropped. Let them drink.

Your impetuous failure to hear, distant-intense,
sense smothered in a bloody knowingness.

Apart

Life dies in air and light:
a fish pulled from the stream,
knife-bright anguish gasping
as if to sustain the spasm
of its dying in the dry,
the dream on the rush to die.

A real knife shines in the hand,
or dulls dropped in a river,
like a caught fish in the light
or flung back in where larger
fish move like as at night
the forearm of a lover.

You lower your head and eyelids,
your eyes' once too wild light
have entered too deep a cover
for me to have any sight
now, as knife you dull and lie,
my arm will not move over.

Blood on the Moon

Somewhere between the blue
and the black half-light,
in mutual pain give birth to
your child to the fear still living
you bide with still out of fear –
what life to be hers could you give her,
watery prey to the same
dark stars in whose movement
you are, owning barely your name?

Without them you'd feel the sad air
or water you with them are,
that are your hope and despair,
whose deaths seem your own self's murder
rather than the dying to live
which alone it's been said might save her.

Bardykes

(a bing by Blantyre)

Silver birches on a black hill,
many a generation frozen, white
waves again ready to,
soldiers, assault a summit
none there could ever attain,
call the wind to get behind them,
the ground to sustain their climb;
till chilly winds whisper over
scatters of dust and snow
in which they go, dissolve
standing still. Old,
    their children would run rings round them
    growing up round their feet; no
    menace, mystery, meaning
    for them this place they play in...
    contending, starting, intertwining.
Birches however press their
obsessive un-understanding –
if they could attain the crumbling
summit, there would be nothing.
    Starlight on iron, bones on a battlefield
    far too long under the pulsing of the sun;
the same stand again,
unsatisfied, interminable old-aged adolescence
driving still on the horizon's red flare.

    Under the roses in a garden
    long since deserted by all but young children,
    new shoots slowly come out, are trampled;
    on the bing children running
    strike sparks off clinker, kick them
    into rising gas, then explosion

consumes them, the many
dead mists wreathe, embracing.
Birches, tilted, recover
unaware of what is, red, coal,
whether one and another explosion
will consume these light lives whole.

Held in the heat of time,
gold, silver, flicker
bright and soon extinguished,
flat ash prevails where
senseless birches commemorate
contention, endless, frozen
roots unseen, forgotten –
struggling and not struggling,
    unaware, going round them
    of girl, boy, fostered, seeding
    ground apart from the stand.

Not visible on any face,
feeding on, crumbling to
bright light and ash that will,
froth on the shore, stand,
sheer flotsam, half-scattered,
regathered to a dead calm
sunset reddens to blood,
sending the children home,
leaving the birches behind
slowly growing colder,
floating ghosts of old
vessels time took down,
cutting no foam or wake.
No snakes where for a million
years there never was a hill
till this one piled up confusing the middle of the valley.
Ash, brick red ruins
command a sweep of road
their old life threw off course;
crooked and straight the law,
strong to be always thrawn like an angered adder.

Law sent a gory burn slinking
under the hawthorn through hollows,
a land's forgotten servant
subject to and accepting

what blackly comical birches
try to sclim (mimicking
the Iwo Jima memorial)
over so many flooded channels

deeper than a man could go now,
    Strata there creak, roll, sink,
    logs in the fire, men's bones,
    dead in disorder, a man's
    who died a hero trying
    to bring his brother's, father's, uncle's,
    back; with which his lie now, the numbers
    tarnished off their work-tags.

These fell in a wave
others escaped breathing (who went on elsewhere to die).
Whether it's warm, or chilly like the first air of morning,
one forgotten feature after another
                is hidden under ground, fading to water
where weariness deadens laughter,
              spider and web soundless below a horizon.

Bodies left floating from shipwreck,
                a low sun turning crimson,
about refuse bobbing children   unaware they are moving
on or in any sea, drifting, trampling the land,
on paths with new or old   weeds, grass, overgrown.

Red faces rising up   the hill's bare blind side
on the steep slope of despair   no birch ever knows:
boy, girl, stand on the summit,
              can't but see, still young
for the seeded steep side's vision
of a need to defeat an invincible which will pass.
Boy, girl, grown and older,   no more go so high:
but into the red brick ruins.   Old enough to bear arms
he goes into her body,   under the shattered time-clocks
she takes the weight of his shoulders
           and arms' as yet unfilled power
like the restlessness born of the moon
          of a sea not sick of the lull
mastered entirely naked, each
          covering, clothing, the other.
From these two's infancy the birches   never changed in fine;
Some fell, slipped, some grew stronger,
         put new shoots through and out.

Boy, girl, again two,
uncovered, cold unsteady step
through brown leaves, drifts, to winter,
cold weight of the wind, whose equal
blew on grandfathers' faces, on heads
come red swimming up from the dark,
that fetched up fuel for furnaces
into bleak day or flarelight
from the pit's consistent midnight.
It may blow dust into dew
in the same eyes as back then,
also into children's,
or have blown the day before
on eyes that evening closed,
and on shall swirl without limit,
    ayont sinuous and shadowed,
    leaf beauty, waterway, body,
    cold wind into the burning
    rodent eyes of night's fire,
    stir up the dew of memory
    flickering back sky's light.

    Trees creak like machinery.
    The wind abides, breath blown
    through deep channels
    from dawn breaking red
    when stiff limbs ache
    in scent of light, rest.

ii

For as long as light opens
a face on this earth or closes
eyes taken back to the terror
which dazzles newborn sight
even on a dull day
raw naked alien yelling
    for comfort, the old man
    who that morning long ago
    came to face each relief, each return,
    will grimace in the wind,
    open eyes cracking, flex
    a thick trunk, expel
    night's last air to clear
    his mouth for a cool drink: morning,

first of the day. Deliberate
in movement from length of life,
he'll balance yet, when ready
stand, if precarious, peaceful.

Winter night falls sudden, sinks
into earth with or without him;
abandoned by his burden, gone
without it into the white
mass of the sky, and absence:
seen as light, experienced
in bones' balance –
loneliness, freedom.
The wind continues,
ruffles the scalp of day,
leaves on trees, on the ground,
forgotten rags of clothing,
puddles, planks, loose bricks, dust.
        Sniff earth in the dull of
        slurry, air, stink of tarnish,
        starvation, the silver of time,
        white wooden hearts or birches;
        the old man's prime still isn't
        entirely away, smiles, lingers.
        Beside it, iron will, Judas,
        is just just stupid.

Sat on a green hill he takes
a tot from his bottle in a dirty shelter
then goes home sweaty to wash down his body;
he falls asleep, sleeps on.
Earth's face is green, that can move.
Naked, awake, his grandson
sings the sky through twenty years' birches
he chases off with the black of time immemorial.
        The girl's bare white sitting up,
        half-covered by her hands, half in shadow:
        the dawnbow sky says what will be, colours to be born,
        the whole breadth of the valley to fill with sound
        awakening as her own body fills,
        wide sky, earth; sounds, buildings, shadows,
        shoots full though once trodden down,
        the boy a horse tall, brindling ground.

Each in its place a birch
is determined, tree that it is,
neither worse nor better
than what was there before;
each casting sheer black shadow,
this poem on dead wood, ash, and
when sunshine makes birches golden
the neither lover will be there.

So many nights never acknowledged
        as that one's like, only
        bare night with its changes
        and lovers hand in hand
        that night, and those others
        back before human meaning
like the birches' extreme, striving from the first in vain.
No doubts to be mated,
no waking fights, the grandfather
sleeps on, birches go down.

        Lonely birches the colder
        for day's dying, the couple
        avoiding roads and noise,
        wondering eyes and the toiling
        burn's ways twisting, go,
        themselves one more meander,
        growing to down to deep water.
No children came here all day
under the birds' stubborn pretence,
        which isn't patience. Day ripened;
        red-gold by noon, day died.
        Two warm a deserted shelter,
        themselves their final shelter,
        night winds put birches to sleep
        like sighing children; two bodies –
        Aphrodite, the bed of the sea –
        take a weight none holds long,
        the moon and sea-foam clouds,
        shattered, scattering timbers.
        Light again day, the waters
        broke – the grandfather's breath;
        boy, girl, despaired of each other,
        the silver soldiers were blind
        at midnight though gold at noon…
        and again the bloody assault!

Sunlight or moonlight as one
to them, degrees of light,
who couldn't fall back as lovers
will, sun on their skin...
forever have been, sea lapping white,
still are and will be birches.

On a black hill nails,
dawn weariness quieting
scratchy twigs, buds
from the first beginning's black
burst at last, spring beyond life and nothing,
loam gold as the sun after the burial,
the flicker of rose through the digging
no frozen intricate principle of the birches.

Personal Note

You want a language expressive
of feelings I'd have jettisoned,
flung as so much rubbish
that self-ignites, on the bonfire.

You hint at a communion
when I'd be not all alone
but unable to catch up with
your quickening confusions.

You tell me to be human,
state that what I care for
is dead, I should say other,
do other (be as you are?).

A party of manipulations,
'kisses and horrid strife'
and not 'the obscene ego' –
more life but not my life?

That I was wrong to love
a you you would be no longer
is what I cannot know,
but I could not not care.

Out of Order

This thing they had sighted seemed steady,
though a ship afloat, as an island.
Mud-heavy level, becalmed,
she met each wave of wash with a thud.

Each rise as they drifted nearer
gave clearer sight; ordered silent,
each bump of a ripple more deadly
than, engines stopped, their heartbeats,
and behind-hand mouthed ironies swelled
in the mid-ocean calm to the cawing
of something delighted by carrion,
and killed by a word like God's,
whose echo gave clearer intensity
to each detail seen of the vessel,
and to the shock as her crew crept out
from wherever they had been below.

A boarding party – not resisted
or welcomed – found her dirty engines sound,
erupted they worked as they were meant to.
Nothing was wrong with the steering.
The crew were examined, were healthy,
were well provisioned, had water.
There was fuel, cargo (slag) in both holds.
They said nothing to be interpreted,
no papers could be discovered
but she had her complement of officers.
It might have been one of them, or a rating,
during the night cut the tow.

No party had been stationed aboard,
no return search was feasible, aircraft
asked for by the disobliging radio
flew over, returned without sighting.

She might as well have been on the bottom.
Inquiries may proceed on the basis
of her name and port, this poem
omits nothing else known as known.

The Slater

The window's crisp diamante
signals a room too damp, too icy,
for any sleeper's good;
sat high, calm, thick-wrapped strolling,
its stillness seems the stability
and overcoat warm of some homes.

Animation minimised, maybe
never to be restored,
the speug-brown slater couldn't live
knocked off skirting this cold,
whose unmoving exoskeleton
wandering fancies to be trembling,
which it can't be, not a mammal.

Plaything of heat, cold, dark,
the light it quietly shies from,
damp, dirt, its forebears survived in,
mystery best at a modest distance
is not what it lives in, or signals
it lives in, signalling quietly
to some slight lear of history.

Street lights colour ice yellow
that is a crust on windowpanes
the thick-wrapped walker can fancy
better than water thaw sends
running from ice's denying
sight of children chittering blue.

Humans creak at the joints,
crottle like roof-snow gathered
to limbs on the gutters half-toppled,
ache, might well not survive
echoes of coughs which do
shake the slater on the wall.

Plaster stuck dust, black timber
paint-resistant with water,
this dump's going back to an earth
whose soft decay's suspended
by half-holds like the frozen
slater's which I wish well.

Apres une Audition de Liszt

The *Jeux d'Eaux'* precarious balance
risks the glassy summit
where fear haunts any movement,
life a sometime play of blizzards
flung in the face through fingers
to terror, a keyboard exploding...

Holding themselves, advancing,
till the rare air kills both dread
and ratiocination –
fingers alive without want
of security, want of life –
and marries and renders fecund the high isolation.

The chest no longer breathless
fills expels and feels the air pour through it
as the summit emerges through dazzle in its light.
The bridges lightly builded are in plain sight.
Returning below the land was always blessed
even in winter. Yet the cold can kill.

These almost airless spaces are breathing
strong as the ploughman's heart. No longer seeing
the crossings between the peaks not past forgetting
the spirit rediscovered in their traverse
an order not emotion's or calculation's,
which discovered free of aspiration is.

Let Licht

... lift up your heid, love,
your een are ti scan wi,
descry difficult things
as weel's see the simple,
be simple, giein you licht,
no as gin they were sheenin
divine wi loe and showin
the empty shell wi the whilk
sheer feelin baurs grouwin.
That they gie thae same looks blinns them.

Like a dark warld only beginnin,
yon ane whaur ill dreams confine them –
let there be licht, sen creation
happent lang syne, the Faa,
and the Christ's resurrection, ava.

Preliminaries

Roughed-out wash, grey waking
raw over the sea, sky low,
birds blurred to seeing squalling
cold out and in, their wings
cover sleep, chill uncover –
flailing as they tailspin off –
hunger for sleep, food, comfort,
dead of a shore sheer rock.

It feels late, but is winter,
and somewhere within the wait
of this wild sky slow to colour
focus: this is a haze,
I see the relentless thin-ness
real things seem lost to subliming,
the dew-frost's surface pure white
expire, and find patience with time.

ii

That northern sea which this morning
sustains my living, wakens scent
of the calm come once old life's crumbled,
calm borne ashore by rough daylight's
wash through my room.

Like eyes dazzled wide, the sky –
which has not had time to colour –
spreads an easy grey like the blanket
on me and like the sleep
still in and about my body.

I watch lights out at sea still blinking
remind me or strengthen memory,
and watch from astern the ferry
on the flat midwinter ebb chuggingly go.

But only from where I'm watching,
nothing is at this moment
receding, the turn is only
detail of the calendar
nothing to where how who and what we are.

Ontario Requiem

i

Not enough life left even for himself,
things demanded of him he worked to give
till he could no more be here; he lost health,
the things in him which had simply to live
to let him be were stifled; not let be,
he lost all feel of here, poisoned the place
was, for him – green glossed over, a corpse face
under a frosted tight and silver sea.

ii Light Like the Mine's Dark...

To deiving light, head reeling
down a mine, blind until
the visible point's discovered,
to light that is and has been here,
whose presence is a meeting,

black overhanging sky delivered
from over sea a miner
who found no rest in the wheel
of no horizon, and *not* exhausted
worked on to the end

without will to evasion
from the caves he was of body,
the brow his thinking was,
heart of him a tree,
he its sometime heart,

sometimes wearer, whiles
clothing, treegrowth trailing,
sometimes drapery hanging,
times bars of a jail
his being and his here here.

A tree too full of summer
sheered burdened with a fruiting
beyond what it could bear
and that rotted unripened
until the snow closed in,
that can shrink to a grimace
its first and only face.

The rock of grief might, torn
away, reveal a newborn
face sticky with birthing,
or a morning red sun burning
on the bones of a man gone down,
that loud unfeeling woman,
bedded stone slow to roll.

iii

A shock of sudden snow...
Under unkempt thick hair
excitement near to a glow
in the light-trembling, boy's, face
reddening to go, like into a sledge-race.

The load of the fall needs shifting
first, from path, street: mounds
to shovel in place by the side
of the clear way, paving, steps, scraped
not to be trodden slippery.

Flurries of breath shift rapid,
the face is swathed against sweat
catching the chill, a lesson
this work as oxygen debt
pains muscles that get stiffer.

A frost of tiredness evenings
on calf back forearm neck,
digging deeper, with stumbling
that's laughed at as a different
lesson by shapes looking on

as if with this all his work
ran like snow melted, his life
thinned back to streaks on the path
that fading now gave no trouble,
thin, grey as his hair, his breath,

unsteady, stuttering student's
in whose pale face what once trembled
could die away joyless, with nothing
now, life thaw to a trickle
off bare stone into mud.

His didn't, and if he vanished
he did live in that sheer white
which leaves no more sign of him
under what, burning, killed him,
a clear sky wild with stars –
nothing of human warmth in
its long night's glittery dark.

iv ... lest...

Ships heave into harbour
laden, as a box drops
they grow lighter in water;
under ground the box stops.
Some silence is due

but not to respect for those
beings who would have silence
too near to a selfish quiescence,
truth sheathed, sin safe,
and the big lie freely spoken...

to the wait not incidental
to the stone's rolling slow
as a wood's growing,
to catch words for other
things, persons, essential.

v Epiphany in Passing
(with thanksgiving for Thomas Merton)

He stood up, having fingered,
that moment he broke from his walk
which had already continued,
one bar of odd, novel chords
just as he'd passed the piano.

He was gone and the chords were singing;
something that won't now be closed
had opened, invisible, spoken,
a moment's blessing that lingered
in this tall North American air.

To the breadth of lake and plain,
wind-rattled prairie, chilled maples'
masses of rosed gold eye fragrance,
and the sky, he bequeathes resonance:

never dead words, those chords
drift more tender than birds,
open space in emptiness, breathing,
live like the shapes of a leaf.

vi The Plateau above Scarboro Bluffs

Trees on a lawn, deck all earth afloat on earth,
above snow thaw – Buddhist-sharpened pinnacled
clay and sand layers, no prow, plough or breaking,
no far shore in sight, here all shoreline, kinglets,
what land holds continuous above the lake.

The dark and crawling things in lately tumbled
apples and walnut fruits not lost entirely
in bents or trodden must flaunt shop conformity;
sour brown crinkled, the hauteur of the unripe
crumbles, the mode, falls away ordinary.

Whoop incarnate an ebon-shining squirrel
shoots, force of joy up the perfect vertical
tall trunk of a fruit-tree to where its branches
with their own light strength will lift above my griefs
still some few separate winter-clinging leafs.

Black Hellebore

Darkened by winter weather's
grubby clumsy handling
the Christmas Rose ignores
bruise and stain. It grows
simply because it can.

None of the world's marbles
can be carved clean to its equal.
It never shrinks with cold,
throws off its shroud of snow
and shows, as of old.